ONE
MORE THING BEFORE YOU
LEAVE
HOME

Patricia E. Basden

All rights reserved by **Patricia E. Basden**. This book or any portion thereof may not be reproduced or used in any manner whatsoever without the expressed written permission of the publisher except for the use of brief quotations in a book review.

ISBN: 978-0-578-39786-3

Distributed by **Power Of Purpose Publishing**

www.PopPublishing.com

Atlanta, Ga. 30326

All rights owned and reserved by **Patricia E. Basden**

Table of Contents

ABOUT THE AUTHOR i

INTRODUCTION ii

CHAPTER 1 1

    What You Need to Know and Have Before Renting

CHAPTER 2 8

    Steps Before You Rent

CHAPTER 3 13

    How To Qualify

CHAPTER 4 15

    What You Should & Should Not Do While Renting

CHAPTER 5 18

    Learn Different Ways to Pay Your Rent

CHAPTER 6 22

    How To Build Your Credit While Renting

CHAPTER 7 25

    Questions To Ask Before Choosing a Roommate

CHAPTER 8 27

    You Want Your Security Deposit Back?

CHAPTER 9 29

    Why The Landlord Won't Renew Your Lease.

CHAPTER 10 31
    TRUE LIFE STORIES
CHAPTER 11 35
    DON'T LIVE ABOVE YOUR MEANS
ACKNOWLEDGEMENTS 38
GLOSSARY 40

ABOUT THE AUTHOR

Patricia E. Basden is a woman on a mission to educate the first-time renter. She isn't a realtor nor is she a licensed real estate attorney. Who is she? She's first and foremost a mother who cares about her young adult daughter's generation. As she believes her own generation should help establish young people towards independence, Ms. Basden created this guide to prepare 18+ year-olds for living decisions they will undertake. She feels settled adults can use this book along with love and guidance, to impact first-timers in planning for this exciting season in their lives.

INTRODUCTION

What is a life skill not taught in high schools but if it were, many young adults would benefit from it? As a 7-year veteran Administrative Assistant & Assistant Property Manager, I have interacted with people of all ages and from all walks of life who were relatively clueless about the fundamentals of renting before signing their first lease. They had no idea of their credit score and lacked crucial information when it came to renewing or ending a lease.

Therefore, I created this guide to outline the basics of the process and the expectations of all parties once they sign on the dotted line. And because the life of the renter is more than paying rent each month, I include suggestions from budgeting to choosing the right roommate.

My Prayer

Father God, we call on You to allow this guide to be purchased and placed in the right hands. May the information enclosed be fully utilized toward the right decision for what will be the reader's next home. May they understand how to live within their means and receive guidance on what they can afford. I ask that they not compare themselves with friends or family, but to know their experience will be uniquely their own. Most importantly, give them the courage to ask all the questions they need, as this can spare them headaches down the road. Fill the reader with strength to stand against the fear that would attack their minds. In your son, Jesus' name, I pray.

Amen!

- CHAPTER 1 -

What You Need to Know and Have Before Renting

Terms in this section:

    Agent

    Amenities

    Efficiency apartment

    First and last month

    Lease agreement

    Management Company

    1b or 2b, 1b with a living room

    Rent

    Renter's Insurance

    Sublet

    Studio apartment

    Security deposit

You believe you're ready to go into the world as an independent adult and rent a room, or 1- or 2-bedroom apartment. Here are some essentials to know before stepping into the arena of renting. Let's start with the questions you must be able to answer before you execute or sign the lease:

Security Deposit and Rent

- Do you have to pay the **1st and last month's rent and security,** or will you be required to pay the real estate **agent's fee** in addition to 1st and security? (The answer can vary depending on the state where you live)

- Does the landlord, management company, or leasing agency require you to have a particular credit score to be eligible to rent?

- How many paystubs or bank statements will you need to submit with your application?

- What is included in the rent? (Ex: cable, or utilities: light water, electricity, or services: trash removal)

- What day is the rent due and how much is the late fee?

- How many days are you allowed to be late with your payment (or length of grace period) before the collections/evictions process is started?

- Are they offering a **month to month, three, six month or annual lease?**

- What happens if you **breach** or break your lease?

- What method of payment can you use to pay your rent? The renter is usually given different payment options. Whatever payment type you choose, maintain a record of your payments, and make sure your receipts state the correct date and paid amount

- Does the landlord require you to have Renter's Insurance? (I highly recommended you purchase this)

Services/ Property Maintenance

- Does the landlord change the AC filter or are you required to do so?

- Who takes care of pest extermination? If they do, find out how often it is scheduled

- Know the recycling and trash schedules (ex: where bins are placed for removal)

- Can you install a Ring doorbell or other wireless security system?

Amenities

- Are a washer and dryer included, or is there an on-site laundry room available, fitness center?

- Does the rental come with parking, and if so, with how many spaces? Is that included in the rent?

- Is property ADA compliant if you or your guests need disability accessibility?

Pets /Human visitors

- Do they allow pets? If yes, how many and what type do they allow?
- Are there restrictions for guests who stay over or about **subletting** your apartment?

Ask yourself

- What size rental suits my needs and what can I afford?
- Is my income at least 3x more than the amount of my rent?

This income to rent ratio assures the owner a tenant can pay rent, especially if an unforeseen event occurs

If you can't answer these questions before you sign the lease, you may end up quickly regretting your decision. Do your research and read all information available about the property (ex: online listings, etc.). Have your specific questions ready for the real estate agent or other person referring the apartment to you. Also don't be intimidated to ask property management or the landlord about terms or rules in the lease you do not understand.

Know Your Rights

It's up to you to be informed about the rights that protect you as a renter in your state *before* you enter into a rental agreement. There are reasons and conditions under which a tenant can legally terminate their lease. In the state of Florida, tenants who are in an unsafe situation created by landlord/management can learn about their protections at http://www.kin.com. (Florida Landlord Tenant Law In A Nutshell.) Find the related site for your state.

Most Important Sections To Understand And Agree To In A Lease

The length of a lease document can vary from 1- 19 pages and should include the topics listed below. If one of these topics or something else important to you is not mentioned in the lease, ask about it before signing the agreement. You can request that your concern be added to the document. Whatever the length of the lease, make sure you fully understand everything covered.

- The parties' (landlord & tenant(s) names are clearly stated
- Length of the lease
- Monthly payment
- What services or amenities are covered in the rent? (This can vary by location)

ONE MORE THING BEFORE YOU LEAVE HOME

- How many pets you can or cannot have and rules on guests and their pets

- Payment required to move in: First, last and security, or agent, last and security. (If you use an agency, this can affect your payment).

- Are you allowed to sublet your space?

- When and if the landlord can enter the property and under what conditions

- Read if the landlord requests you follow certain behavioral rules. For ex: no smoking, playing loud music after a certain hour

- What is the number to report any issues such as A/C not working?

- Signature spaces making the agreement official

- What appliances are included in the rental?

- The following questions may not be mentioned in your lease, but you need to ask and be clear on:

- Are you allowed to paint the walls? Do you need to repaint them their original color before you move out?

- Can a TV be hung on the wall? Are you responsible for repairing the wall before you move?

- Are there designated quiet hours for the property?

- Are there separate rules for guests?

- How much notice does management give before entering the apartment?

- Under what circumstances is management allowed to enter the apartment without my authorization?

- Who does management allow to enter the apartment with prior permission when I'm not present?

- CHAPTER 2 -

Steps Before You Rent

Terms in This Section:

Prorated

Tenant

Walk-through

Now that you know what is included in the rent and you've been approved as a tenant, here are some steps to take and address before officially moving in:

- Make sure the lease rental amount reflects the exact amount you owe for that first month based on the day you move in. If you are moving in on the third, fifth or thereafter of that month, the rent for the month should be **prorated**

- If you choose to pay the rent by money order, it must be completed correctly. Not doing so can cause you problems. (See the Money Order Sample in Chapter 5)

Do your walk-through before you move in and before you move out. Verify the following appliances or fixtures are operational:

- Toilet and all faucets

- Stove and oven
- Heat and A/C
- Refrigerator and freezer for door closure and temperature
- Windows slide up and down
- There are no holes on the walls and floors
- If you notice any of the above items aren't working and you are interested in the property, **DO NOT** wait until *after* you move in to point them out. You can be blamed for their disrepair. Speaking about them up front will also enable you to see how the management responds to residents
- Contact vendors such as electric, cable companies, etc. before moving in, if their services aren't included in your rent
- Complete a Change of Address form online or at the post office
- If you haven't established a good credit history, some vendors may require a deposit for a certain period of time. This fee assures the vendor you will pay for services on a timely basis

ONE MORE THING BEFORE YOU LEAVE HOME

Suggestions

- Purchase a folder organizer or safety deposit box for your rental payment receipts
- Keep a copy of your lease and rental insurance in either suggested item
- Get familiarized with what your lease requires you to do
- Separate your wants from your needs and limit unnecessary spending
- Below is a list of essential items I recommend you save for to avoid using rent money to purchase them. It helps to write down their cost to evaluate if they should be bought now or later
    - Utensils: knives, forks, spoons, $_____
    - Dinner set $_____
    - Napkins $_____
    - Toilet tissue $_____
    - A stockpot $_____
    - A frying pan $_____
    - Four to six cups (plastic or glass) $_____
    - A mop and bucket $_____,
    - A broom and dustpan $_____
    - Bath soap $_____
    - Dishwashing soap $_____
    - Air freshener $_____
    - A blow-up bed $_____

- Bed sheets $_____
- Clothes hangers (12 or 24) $ _____
- 3M Command Picture hanging strips $_____
(To avoid placing holes in the walls.)
- Iron and iron boarding $_____
- Toothpaste & toothbrush $_____
- Cleaning products $_____
(Bleach, laundry detergent, hand sanitizer)
- Towels (4) $_____
- Blankets $_____
- Table and four chairs $_____

If you can't buy all of these at the same time, people have used crates as chairs and bought placemats until they acquired a dining set.

- TOTAL: $_____
- OPTIONAL ITEMS
    Microwave $_____
    Air fryer $ _____
    Lamp $ _____
    Standing Mirror $ _____
    Shoe stand or shoe rack $ _____
    Hairdryer $ _____
    Television $ _____

Helpful tip: **You're Also Renting the Neighborhood**

Your apartment is not limited to the property you'll be spending most of your time in. It's within a neighborhood with businesses and services that will affect your lifestyle for as long as you rent there. I suggest you visit the property at night as well as in the

ONE MORE THING BEFORE YOU LEAVE HOME

day. Get a feel and sense of safety of the environment. If you will be coming home late at night, walks from the bus stop or train station or parking distances, can become a major issue for you. Also consider:

- Your distance from local amenities: grocery, gas station, your job. Do you need a car? Is there reliable public transportation?

- Are there nearby activities which suit your interest?

- Do you feel comfortable walking/driving in the neighborhood? Are neighbors friendly, nosy, standoffish, racist?

- CHAPTER 3 -

How To Qualify

Terms in This Section:

> **Guaranty of Lease Agreement**

If you want to leave home and don't have enough money saved, but your parents are willing to co-sign your rental expenses, some landlords will accept a **Guaranty of Lease Agreement.** This assures the owner that your parent(s) will supplement the portion of the rent you aren't able to pay.

Renting through a leasing agency is an option to consider when you don't have enough savings for first, last and security payments. Leasing agencies usually don't charge these fees and their approval process is significantly quicker than renting directly from a landlord. Another plus is that they are generally willing to allow pets for an additional fee.

The leasing company will almost always offer onsite maintenance with an important condition. You will be required to pay for parking and other amenities and services like sewer, trash, electricity, and cable, separately from your rent.

ONE MORE THING BEFORE YOU LEAVE HOME

ITEMS YOU ARE REQUIRED TO SUBMIT IN ORDER TO QUALIFY FOR THE RENTAL:

- Provide references (personal, educational, professional) who can attest to your character and stability

- Complete a rental application

- Provide paystubs or bank statements

- Proof you receive a scholarship. If you're a college student receiving a scholarship or grant for rent, you may need to provide a copy of the letter stating that

- Your signed agreement permitting your background and credit score to be checked

- CHAPTER 4 -

What You Should & Should Not Do While Renting

Terms in This Section:

> Credit report

> Eviction

Planning Your Payment

You've moved in and are busy making that new place feel like home. Whether you are paid on a weekly or biweekly schedule, know how to allocate a certain dollar amount from each check toward your upcoming rent.

For example, if the rent is $1150.00 per month and you bring home $350.00 per week after taxes, $287.50 from each check should be put toward your rent. Depending on the state you reside in, a percentage of taxes will be deducted from your check leaving you with little to live on. This is one reason to consider staying home a while longer until you are in a stronger financial position.

In another scenario, your rent may be $1250 monthly and you earn $750.00 twice a month. After taxes you should put aside

$625.00. It's important to pay your rent on time to avoid late fees and the eventual collections process that could lead to eviction.

Communicating to the landlord or management company your intention to pay the rent on a specific date (once it is already late), shows your willingness to maintain a positive tenant/landlord relationship. While you'll still be responsible for any late fees, giving them a heads-up may prevent them from expeditiously starting the eviction process.

It is a breach of your lease agreement when you fail to pay your rent in a timely manner. The landlord or leasing company can file eviction papers against you and report your non-payment to credit bureaus: Experian, Equifax, and TransUnion. A negative credit report follows you years into the future and can hinder you from leasing and buying property. Additionally, lenders will require you to pay hefty security fees or higher interest rates on loans when you have an eviction on your record. Some landlords and rental agencies may allow you to explain the reasons for your eviction, but overall, it's an experience you want to avoid.

Repairs

It's your responsibility to immediately document and report to the landlord or management company any issues with fixtures or appliances that came with the apartment: pipes, windows, air conditioner, for example. Do not attempt to fix anything or hire someone to handle the repair without their permission. Doing so opens you up to blame for the malfunction of the item.

Visitors

Advise the landlord when friends or family are staying more than three to five days. You may not think it's important, but water and electricity usage may slightly increase during their visit. Management may require you to pay extra to the rent to offset this increase.

Check your state's laws regarding long-term guests, particularly if the lease agreement doesn't include rules about this. In some states, a guest or visiting relative can be considered a tenant after a certain period of time. Should someone refuse to leave your home, you will be forced to pay for the eviction process (financially and emotionally) to get them to leave.

Also be wise about allowing a family member or friend to receive mail at your home. A mailing address can be considered proof of residency and work against you if you must resort to legally removing them.

- CHAPTER 5 -

Learn Different Ways to Pay Your Rent

Be aware that if you sign a month-to-month lease agreement, the landlord can increase the rent at any time. Your state may not have rent increase control laws allowing the landlord to raise the rent at will. If your state doesn't offer this protection, find out the number of days in advance of your rent when it can be increased.

Once you're clear on these points, know the rental payment methods used in your state and those accepted by management.

Payment Methods:

- **CashApp -** Free mobile banking app
- **Zelle -** Digital payment platform for receiving and sending money
- **Personal Check -** Provided by your banking institution. It uses the bank routing and account numbers to process your rent
- **Cashier's Check –** This is considered as good as cash. You can purchase these guaranteed checks from your

- **Cash** – In the event you're unable to purchase a money order or cashier's check, or do not yet have a bank account, this may be your best option. But protect yourself by obtaining a receipt when you hand over the cash. Do not leave the payment center without this proof of payment UNDER ANY CONDITION

- **Money Order** – Like the cashier's check, this method is considered guaranteed money. Money orders can vary in their appearance, but they require the same information to be valid. See the instructions and sample below:

The sections you are required to confirm and fill in are:

1) Date of the money order   (confirm)
2) The correct amount being paid   (*confirm*)

ONE MORE THING BEFORE YOU LEAVE HOME

3) The dollar amount written in words   (*confirm*)

4) Person or company receiving the payment as stated in your lease agreement. Write that name on the line: "Pay to or Pay To The Order Of"   (*Fill in*)

5) If your money order has the section: "Purchaser Address" or "From Address" write your address (*Fill in*)

6) Print your name on the line *above* "Signature," and then sign *underneath* your printed name   (*Fill in*) Note: *postal money orders only require your written name. Most others have a signature line*

7) If there is a "memo" section write the month & year the payment is covering

8) The perforated side (can be to the left) or bottom portion of the money order is your receipt. In case there is a discrepancy about if you made the payment (or when you made it), this portion will serve as proof of payment and date

9) If the landlord states the money order wasn't received, the establishment you purchased it from can use the numbers printed on the perforated section to investigate if the order has been cashed

10) Most importantly, DO NOT sign the back of the money order. Only the name listed on the "Pay To The Order Of" line (landlord), is to sign or endorse your rent payment

ENCOURAGEMENT

Chapter 6 includes strategies to build your credit score once you obtain your rental. However, if you don't have the credit score needed to rent in the state you will be residing in, there are other avenues available to you:

- Search for direct landlord rental properties

- Limit your search to rentals that require three to six months proof of income. Know that landlords prefer prospective renters with an income three times above the rental amount

- Inquire if they will allow you to pay two security deposits

- Ask one of your friends with a stronger credit score if they are willing to rent with you. (Read Chapter 7 Questions To Ask Before Choosing A Roommate)

- Depending on the real estate market and inflation rates, leasing companies may offer "move in specials." These specials may not include a specific credit score as a requirement for renting

- CHAPTER 6 -

How To Build Your Credit While Renting

As this is your first rental, you will want to build your credit score for future rentals or ownership investments. There are platforms and businesses to keep you informed and on the upward track with your credit.

- Experian Boost allows you to connect your utility payments as a means of increasing your credit score. Although you may join Experian Boost, this will not impact your Transunion or Equifax credit scores. However, improving your score on even one of the credit bureaus can only benefit you

- Research what constitutes a good credit score for your state

- Know the vendors you pay your utilities to, will report your poor or nonpayment patterns to credit bureaus as quickly as the person/company who receives your rent

- Learn how your credit/charge card usage is reflected on your credit report. Keep in mind if you apply and obtain a secure credit card, you will be required to give a deposit to the issuing agency

- Future landlords/management will contact your present landlord to learn about your payment history and about your overall behavior as a tenant

Digital Resources

- John S. Kiernan breaks down the six types of credit cards on *WalletHub*, the personal finance website. Check it out to know which ones you should avoid and the best way to use the ones you need. Effective and mature management of your credit cards can also strengthen your credit score

- There are also social media sites that dispense valuable information on personal finances like FACEBOOK's, *The Budgetnista* by Tiffany Aliche. Aliche is a great financial educator who presents strategies on credit building with doses of inspiration. No matter what tools you use to increase your credit standing, you will be empowering your present and future with a financially responsible reputation

- Pay attention to digital, print publications or media that offer personal financial advice. An article I recommend is in the newsletter, *Next Advisor in Partnership With Time,* featuring "Reporting Your Rent" by Ryan Haar, dated March 31, 2021. Haar explains how paying your rent on schedule enhances your credit standing

Programs that report your payments to credit bureaus

- Experianboost
- RentBureau
- Rent Kharma
- RentReporters sends information to Experian
- LevelCredit reports to TransUnion and Equifax

The state you rent in can help determine the best reporting agency for you to use. You will pay a fee, but it's important to obtain a commitment from the rental management company that they'll respond to the notifications from the agency you select. They then report your monthly payments so your credit standing accurately reflects your payment habits. The article offers suggestions on how to ask your landlord to cooperate with this monitoring tool.

- CHAPTER 7 -

Questions To Ask Before Choosing a Roommate

If you find paying your rent is a struggle and your lease has no restrictions on roommates, please do the following:

- Interview at least three or more potential roommates and ask specific questions about regular guests and visitors, particularly boy or girlfriends who might sleep over

- Discuss the expectations about cleanliness, household chores, food and sharing of any personal items

- Ask about their employment to determine if their portion of the rent can be counted on

- State and inquire about all faith practices so neither of you offend each other

- Write down the answers to all questions to weigh the qualities of the individuals you're considering for a roommate

- Speak to other people who know the individual well. Here are some questions you should include in addition to those you'll come up with on your own:

- Will they accept your rules about sleepover guests? (Ex: length of stay & possible contribution to rent)

- Do they have a girlfriend or boyfriend/partner?

- How will you handle the grocery bill and guests who come over to eat?

- Ask that potential roommate what their family and friends consider to be their flaws and how they are improving them: ex: messiness, bad temper

- Do they have friends who come over late? Are you both morning or night people?

- Would they be against opening a joint account just for rent, utilities, and food? *(You want to know the person very well before taking this step)*

- Do they smoke, drink, do recreational drugs at all or often?

- Do they have a pet or need a service animal? How many? Do they have set rules and methods for taking care of that pet?

- Do they understand the terms of the lease and the consequences of breaching it?

- CHAPTER 8 -

You Want Your Security Deposit Back?

Here are actions that can almost guarantee you'll get your security deposit back:

- When preparing to move from your rental, find the video or pictures you took during your first **walk-through** before you moved there. Compare them with the video and pictures of your final walk-through

- You should have all your items in boxes and ready to move before the next month. This way, the landlord or management cannot hold you responsible for the next month's rent, based on the date you agreed to move

- Inquire what time your walk-through will take place. Afterwards, ask for a copy of your walk-through document to learn if you've been assigned responsibility for any repairs

- Be mindful of fixtures that fall, or which suffer from **wear and tear** over time like the carpet, and other items used in that property. Your landlord should allow for a reasonable amount of wear and tear if you've rented for 2 years or more

- It's wise to keep this walk-through report until you receive your security deposit. If you don't receive your security deposit within the time you were told, you may need to present this document in court to win a judgment against the landlord

- Inquire how long it will take for you to receive your deposit and when you can expect it

- CHAPTER 9 -

Why The Landlord Won't Renew Your Lease.

You are nearing the end of your lease agreement and are looking forward to signing the new lease. However, management has notified you it will not be renewed. Here are possible reasons:

- Nuisance- During your tenancy you may have had altercations that required intervention from law enforcement or grounds security. Loud music, excessive partying, or extreme noisiness when most people are sleeping, will label you a nuisance. Barking and other noises from your pets at odd hours, or for long periods of time, can render you an undesirable tenant

- Consistent late or nonpayment of rent

- Violating no smoking guidelines

- Abuse of property

- It's been recorded you have high foot traffic and you're suspected of operating an illegal business

ONE MORE THING BEFORE YOU LEAVE HOME

- Neighbors lodged numerous complaints about your lifestyle encroaching on their space

- You never reported any repair issues you had with the property

- The owner has decided to sell the property and the new owners do not want renters

- The landlord/management wants to substantially increase the rent to reflect the market price

- CHAPTER 10 -

TRUE LIFE STORIES

This chapter shares true stories three young adults shared with me about their first rental experience. I've included different experiences to prepare you that being a tenant entails much more than signing a lease.

"Michaela"

A friend connected 23-year-old Michaela to another of her friends who wanted to rent the master suite of his home. The landlord requested she pay the first month's rent, but not the last or a security deposit. Michaela believes because she and the landlord shared a mutual friend, this was the main reason she wasn't given a lease.

They verbally agreed she'd pay $500.00 on a month-to-month basis which included utilities. Michaela bought her own food and laundry detergent, had access to the owner's laundry area and enjoyed occasional visits from friends.

Her finances were jeopardized when a car accident caused her to lose her job. She responsibly gave the owner a 30-day notice and returned home after 6 months of renting. The only other issue before the accident was the property's serious rodent and roach infestation problem. While Michaela wouldn't recommend anyone rent without a written agreement, she admits she only stayed there as long as she did to prove she could live on her own to her family.

"Nayda"

20-year-old Nayda drove to apartment buildings in desirable neighborhoods and asked about their rental requirements and credit scores for prospective renters. She finally found an apartment which only required her to pay the first and last by cashier or personal check.

Although Nayda signed a 12-month lease, she admits she never understood the late fee process. After some time had passed, the management company notified her she had a 3-day grace period to make payment before accumulating a late fee. While Nayda was renting, she reported problems with her A/C as well as a bug infestation.

During her six-month tenancy, her mother became ill, and she had to return home. When Nayda informed the management office of having no choice but to breach the lease, they refused to return her security deposit and penalized her by forcing her to pay 2 months' rent.

"Elijah"

23-year-old Elijah was nervous about the rental process but was relieved when a family member had to break their lease and allowed him to take it over.

Unlike Michaela and Nayda, Elijah had an extensive lease that restricted his behavior. When he read the agreement, he went through each line and prepared his questions for management. He also did a walk-through and brought attention to the items needing repair. He cautions new renters to remember the lease agreement is a legal document and if a landlord takes issue with your questions before you sign, that may not be the tenant arrangement for you.

He urges new renters to be as educated as possible before going into an agreement and to document every issue and interaction after moving in. In addition, he had to rethink some of the guests he allowed to visit especially if their behavior or regard for his space was in question.

Elijah also learned the importance of spending wisely and distinguishing his wants from his needs. He kept records to protect himself from being blamed for future repairs. Other concerns he suggests you be aware of:

- Security provided to protect you and the property
- Frequency of police activity on the property/ in the neighborhood

ONE MORE THING BEFORE YOU LEAVE HOME

- How long it takes for property lights to be replaced
- How you report unsafe areas on the property
- Rules about guest usage of property amenities
- How management handles tenant complaints
- How management handles false complaints against you

Overall, each story offers a different perspective on the factors to consider before renting. Michaela and Nayda's experiences prove the importance of having and understanding a lease, and the awareness of additional fees that can be assigned to you. Their stories remind us how emergencies can impact your ability to come up with the rent. Elijah presented cautions and advice so you can be as prepared as much as possible.

I suggest you become familiarized with the questions in this guide. Once you feel knowledgeable enough and have sufficient finances, you will need to plan and budget for the apartment you can afford.

- CHAPTER 11 -

DON'T LIVE ABOVE YOUR MEANS

Don't Live Above Your Means

Designer items are high priced and healthy food is significantly more expensive than comfort food. It goes without saying the most desirable zip codes are beyond costly for even more established adults. Below are major considerations to make about how you live as a renter, while preparing for your future.

Tips on Wise Spending

Since property owners make tenant decisions largely based on their credit score, you shouldn't use a credit card to purchase items above your pay scale and if you will owe more than 30% of the credit balance. While I acknowledge the importance of having what you need and being comfortable, I suggest you have a plan and a working budget long before you leave home.

Save cash if there is a must have item you want. But in this age with information in the palm of your hand, there are significant bargains to be found if you take the time to research them. Outlet stores and well-made items can provide you with necessary and good-looking imitations while being friendlier to your pocketbook.

Be cautioned against spending for personal items or for your home based on the ideas or tastes of others. This will only leave you stressed and unable to enjoy the purchases you've gone into debt to acquire.

Eating healthy doesn't have to come at a total sacrifice of your wallet. Find farmers' markets (often operating on weekends) in your area or check supermarket ads, to find desired grocery items on sale. Also compare prices of buying in bulk as opposed to buying in smaller sizes, providing it will not go to waste.

Creativity and resourcefulness can go a long way in saving money and making your home comfortable and a reflection of your independence. Many savvy shoppers combine thrift or bargain store fashions with higher end items and are well presented in their professional and personal lives. Between social media and the Internet, people have saved money and increased their sense of self-esteem by developing useful DIY skills.

You may also need to utilize your God given talents and abilities to find a temporary side hustle or to create a business. This could lead you to a more spacious apartment and even fast track you to owning your own home.

Saving

Remember there is always the possibility of losing your job for reasons beyond your control. Emergencies can occur in an instant and change your lifestyle. Therefore, a rainy-day savings fund you put into regularly, should not be used for kicking it with the boys, getting your hair and nails done, or fine dining.

It's a good habit to have a savings goal of three or more months of funds for life's emergencies. This way you give yourself breathing room to take a month to job or apartment search. If your emergency will impact your ability to pay rent, you need to communicate this honestly with your landlord. If you've been a reliable and agreeable tenant, they may be willing to work with you for a while.

Large Purchases

Also carefully consider large credit purchases (autos, certain electronics, and appliances) which take 3 or more years to pay off. Remember they also require money to maintain. Purchases like these need to be planned and budgeted for ahead of time and for as long as you own them.

ACKNOWLEDGEMENTS

I would like to thank the people instrumental in the creation of this guide. My lovely daughter, Jasmin Lewis Pierre, who represents my target audience, eagerly read this information from the beginning. Thanks, Jasmin, for the late nights and for being my sounding board.

I would like to thank realtor extraordinaire, JoAnne Jones, for her valuable insight.

I'm grateful to my niece, Jalecea Ellington, for reading the draft and sharing her positive feedback.

My cousin Elijah Mackey along with Michaela Jean-Baptiste and Nayda Prieto, shared their rental experiences with the heart to help others. Thank you!

I also thank Alexandra Taveras for her impactful feedback that enabled me to write the remainder of this guide.

I thank children's author Patricia Gordon of the WORD SANCTUARY, LLC for her editorial services.

Yummo Bucko Jamel Spalding, I thank you for your generous encouragement when I needed it most.

I am extremely grateful to all the friends and acquaintances who continued to encourage me to finish this guide. They saw the need as I have in preparing the next generation for their independence and success.

GLOSSARY

Agent Fee – This is when the landlord hires a company to take care of the rental process on their behalf. (This will vary by the state you reside in).

Amenities - This can be the fitness center, pool, clubhouse, tennis courts on a property.

Breach of Contract- When one party of the agreement refuses to comply with terms stated in the lease agreement. Ex: a tenant pays the rent after the due date stated in the lease.

Credit Report: A statement that contains all your credit card transactions. This statement shows your responsibility in making credit card payments on time. Leasing companies, landlords, car dealers, banks and other lenders must request your permission to run your report as part of the application process.

Credit Score: This is a scale that categorizes credit history based on bill payment. Strong credit scores can qualify someone for lower interest rates.

Efficiency Apartment - A single room with a kitchenette, living room and dining area with a separate bathroom that is a little larger than a studio.

Eviction: A landlord or other agent legally files with the court to have a tenant removed from the property. Failure to pay rent is the major cause of evictions. Tenants who conduct illegal actions on the premises can also be evicted.

Execute-When both parties agree and sign to acknowledge they will abide by the terms of the contract.

First month's payment - The payment for the first month you move in.

Guaranty of Lease- This agreement assures the landlord a parent or someone else will pay the rent if the tenant is unable to.

Last month's payment - The last month of rent to be paid before you move out. (Do not assume you can use this to pay your rent unless you and the landlord agree).

Month to Month lease-This is a short-term lease. Often the landlord charges a hefty price because there is no guarantee the tenant will continue to rent.

Renters Insurance: The insurance renters purchase to cover damages or theft of personal items occurring in the apartment during the time of the lease. Tenants cannot rely on the landlord's homeowner's insurance to compensate for their losses.

Security Deposit: This fee is used to cover any damages that are possibly made by the tenant.

Studio- An open area in which dining, living room, kitchen and bedroom are all in one.

ONE MORE THING BEFORE YOU LEAVE HOME

Subletting- The tenant has authorization to rent a part of their living space to another tenant/roommate.

Tenant- An individual who pays rent to reside on a property.

Wear and tear: When a tenant consistently uses items in the property, such as carpeting or door handles. These are not to be deducted from your security deposit when you are moving from the property.

2b/1b and living room- Two bedrooms, one bathroom and living room area. This is the preferred living space for the new renter if finances are in order.

3 or 6 month lease: - Short term lease options

12 month lease - The lease option landlords prefer as it assures them of regular income.

www.ingramcontent.com/pod-product-compliance
Lightning Source LLC
Chambersburg PA
CBHW072039060426
42449CB00010BA/2342